NOV   2007

DATE DUE

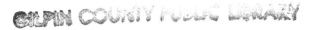

Dogs

Mutts

by Jody Sullivan Rake

Consulting Editor: Gail Saunders-Smith, PhD

Consultant: Jennifer Zablotny, DVM
Member, American Veterinary Medical Association

Capstone press
Mankato, Minnesota

Pebble Books are published by Capstone Press,
151 Good Counsel Drive, P.O. Box 669, Mankato, Minnesota 56002.
www.capstonepress.com

1 2 3 4 5 6 12 11 10 09 08 07

Library of Congress Cataloging-in-Publication Data
Rake, Jody Sullivan.
    Mutts / by Jody Sullivan Rake.
    p. cm.—(Pebble Books. Dogs)
    Summary: "Simple text and photographs present an introduction to mutts, their
growth from puppy to adult, and pet care information"—Provided by publisher.
    Includes bibliographical references and index.
    ISBN-13: 978-1-4296-0016-3 (hardcover)
    ISBN-10: 1-4296-0016-0 (hardcover)
    1. Mutts (Dogs)—Juvenile literature. I. Title. II. Series.
SF427.R237 2008
636.7—dc22   2006100687

Note to Parents and Teachers

The Dogs set supports national science standards related to life
science. This book describes and illustrates mutts. The images
support early readers in understanding the text. The repetition of
words and phrases helps early readers learn new words. This book
also introduces early readers to subject-specific vocabulary words,
which are defined in the Glossary section. Early readers may need
assistance to read some words and to use the Table of Contents,
Glossary, Read More, Internet Sites, and Index sections of the book.

Table of Contents

Marvelous Mix

A mutt is a mix of
two or more
breeds of dogs.
Its father is one breed
and its mother is another.

Some mutts have
their own names.
A pug and beagle mix
is called a puggle.

radio flyer___80

From Puppy to Adult

Mutt puppies
from the same litter
are about the same size.

Mutts grow into different sizes.
A mutt's size depends on the size of its parents.

Mutts can be all colors. They are usually a mix of their parents' colors.

Taking Care of Mutts

Mutts need food, water, and exercise every day. Large mutts need more exercise than small dogs.

Visits to the vet
keep mutts healthy.
Mutts with floppy ears
need them cleaned often.

Mutts make good pets. You can adopt a mutt from an animal shelter.

Mutts look different,
but they all need
love and attention.

Glossary

adopt—to take as one's own; you can adopt a dog from an animal shelter.

animal shelter—a place for homeless animals

attention—playing, talking, and spending time with someone or something

breed—a type of dog

healthy—fit and well, not sick

litter—a group of animals born at one time to the same mother

vet—a doctor that takes care of animals

Read More

Bozzo, Linda. *My First Dog.* My First Pet Library From the American Humane Association. Berkeley Heights, N.J.: Enslow, 2007.

Einhorn, Kama. *My First Book About Dogs.* Sesame Subjects. New York: Random House, 2006.

Internet Sites

FactHound offers a safe, fun way to find Internet sites related to this book. All of the sites on FactHound have been researched by our staff.

Here's how:

1. Visit *www.facthound.com*

2. Choose your grade level.

3. Type in this book ID **1429600160** for age-appropriate sites. You may also browse subjects by clicking on letters, or by clicking on pictures and words.

4. Click on the **Fetch It** button.

FactHound will fetch the best sites for you!

Index

Word Count: 131
Grade: 1
Early-Intervention Level: 16

Editorial Credits

Becky Viaene, editor; Juliette Peters, set designer; Kim Brown, book designer;
Kara Birr, photo researcher; Karon Dubke, photographer; Kelly Garvin, photo stylist

Photo Credits

Capstone Press/Karon Dubke, 12, 14, 16, 18, 20; Cheryl A. Ertelt, cover; Dreamstime.com/
Steven Tan, 6; Ron Kimball Stock/Renee Stockdale, 4; Ron Kimball Stock/Ron Kimball, 8;
Shutterstock/Laura Aqui, 1; Stephen Stromstad, 10

Capstone Press thanks the Kind Veterinary Clinic in Saint Peter, Minnesota, and
dog trainer Martha Diedrich, for their assistance with this book.